CRADLE AND ALL

CRADLE AND ALL

Everything for Welcoming the New Baby

PAMELA SCURRY

Photographs by Elizabeth Zeschin

Text by Catherine Calvert

CLARKSON POTTER/PUBLISHERS

NEW YORK

Dedicated to my mother and father, who shared their joy of life, and to my own "babies," Richardson and Kristina, and to their father, my husband, Richard, all of whom I cherish

Published by Clarkson N. Potter, Inc., 201 East 50th Street, New York, New York 10022. Member of the Crown Publishing Group.

CLARKSON N. POTTER, POTTER, and colophon are trademarks of Clarkson N. Potter, Inc.

Manufactured in Japan

Library of Congress Cataloging-in-Publication Data

Scurry, Pamela.
Cradle and all: everything for welcoming the new baby / Pamela Scurry ; photographs by Elizabeth Zeschin.
p.   cm.
1. Infants—United States.   2. Infants' supplies—United States.
3. Showers (Parties) I. Title.
HQ774.S4 1992

649′.122—dc20
91-25269
CIP

ISBN 0-517-57560-4
10 9 8 7 6 5 4 3 2 1
First Edition

Page 8: Photograph of Catherine Taich

ACKNOWLEDGMENTS

A new baby brings out the best in everyone, and I have many friends to thank for giving their best to this project.

My extra special thank-yous go to Deborah Geltman and Gayle Benderoff, my tireless agents, who went above and beyond a million times over. Thanks, too, to Elizabeth Zeschin, who showed grace, talent, and caring for this book; Catherine Calvert, who lent her gifted writing skills to the text; Lauren Shakely, who encouraged, stretched, molded, and yet let me be who I am; Wendy Palitz, whose design transformed the book into a special treasure; Howard Klein, whose art direction has always been in keeping with the spirit of this book; and Kim Freeman, whose styling started the project on its way.

Many behind-the-scenes participants must be gratefully acknowledged: Dr. William Ledger and The New York Hospital–Cornell Medical Center and Myra Manners, who shared their facilities; and Dr. Patricia Allen, who believes as I do that the birth of each new baby is a new miracle. The entire staff of Camp Greystone helped make our outdoor christening possible, and I am grateful for their cheerful assistance.

I particularly appreciate the willingness of the families and mothers who agreed to be photographed: Sarah Taich and her mother, Mrs. Lile (The Shower); Elizabeth, Peter, and big brother Kyle Keyloun (The Arrival); Katie and Jim Warrington, the grandparents Libby and Jim Miller, Edith Holt and Kacky Keyton, "Jim Boy" and Stuart Miller, Constance Barkley, Starr Teel, Davy Mallett, Christy, and Lisa (The Welcome); Jeanne and John Stewart, parents of Keara, and big brother, Sean, and Dale Lamberty, who made the best first birthday cake ever (The First Birthday); Belinda Haas, mother of Oona; Amy Guttman, mother of Zoë; and Katherine Sill, mother of the sailor baby just learning to walk, William Brown.

Without Harold and Hannah, I could not have managed all the ups and downs. Bob Carbone and Frederic both contributed their spectacular pastry-making talents. Jean Taniguchi helped produce the directory. And all of the staff members at the Wicker Garden and the Wicker Garden's Baby encouraged, held the lights, ironed, carried, and answered far too many calls. I thank them all and the too-many-to-be-named helpers who made my dream of a book on the new baby a reality.

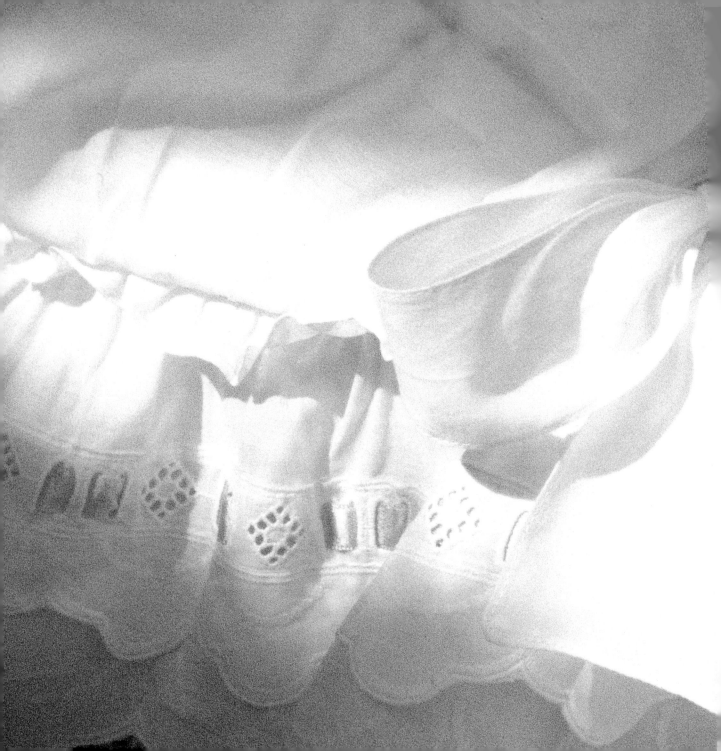

CONTENTS

INTRODUCTION

"Just an ordinary miracle," wrote the English writer Laurie Lee of his new daughter's birth, and his words capture the first rare moments familiar to all parents around the world. There is nothing quite like a new baby, and nothing quite like the headlong rush of love you feel as you look, and look again, at the small perfection in your arms. Mother and father know that ahead lie sleepless nights and weepy days, mountains of wash, and endless miles pushing a stroller, but here, now, in the first few hours of a baby's life, all such concerns are erased in the quiet contemplation of a miracle.

Preparing for a baby's birth is one of life's most pleasurable tasks: readying the nursery, filling the drawers with tiny undershirts and small socks, buying the first small teddy bear or stuffed doll. By making these preparations we ready ourselves, too, for the big change in our lives that will have more to do with how we think of our family than where we shift the furniture.

Certainly during the months of preparation there will be good-natured arguments about a name—and, not least, there will be some moments spent alone in the nursery, imagining the child on its way. And then the baby's here, and you find it impossible to imagine life before her arrival. Days are remade, marked with new borders, new demands, new pleasures, and your old life vanishes like last week's dreams. You watch her blue eyes roam a new world; you watch the small fingers unfurl and reach; you listen as her cries turn to coos and her flailings find momentum and meaning. Little girl, little boy, each begins to chart her or his own universe, within the boundaries you have drawn. What will they remember later on? The organdy curtains you made to filter the bright sun? The clown doll a favorite uncle tucked into a corner of the crib? And mothers and fathers begin to fill their own memories with images great and small—the first step, the first tooth, or simply the glorious sight of a sleeping baby, arms flung wide, as if ready to embrace the world.

Babies are the occasion for celebrations, too—the happy anticipation that a shower brings, the solemn joys of a religious welcoming ceremony, the pride and happiness of a birthday party. By celebrating together, we reinforce those bonds that link us, parent to child, friend to friend, generation to generation, and provide not only happy memories and an album filled with pretty pictures, but the very background against which our child lives his life. Many of our treasured traditions are founded in the customs of our Victorian and Edwardian grandparents—the engraved cards to announce a new birth, the christening gowns of white lawn and delicate lace, the carefully kept diaries of baby's first year, the silver cups with rattles and bits of heirloom jewelry with which we commemorate such a happy occasion. By bequeathing Grandmother's locket to a new baby, we join our child to all those who have gone before, and to everything the family reveres and values, and this is, perhaps, the most important gift to give a young child. I have seen, too, the great pleasure everyone takes in giving a new baby something extraordinary—a handpainted rocking chair or a precious

pottery figure that will become, in its turn, an heirloom for the next generation to enjoy.

"Loveliness beyond completeness / Sweetness distancing all sweetness / Beauty all that beauty may be . . ." wrote one Victorian poet of his new baby. I hope this little book will serve as a wise companion, full of inspiration and information, as you begin this journey with your own source of sweetness and beauty.

THE SHOWER

For generations the baby shower has been the way to share the expectant mother's joy and to begin to fill the baby's nursery. Although some hostesses now extend shower invitations to men as well as women, the traditional women-only shower allows female friends to share their unique understanding of motherhood. Guests usually include the closest relatives and friends of the mother-to-be. A luncheon at home is an ideal occasion for chatting and opening the gifts for all to see.

Just because the shower celebrates a baby's imminent arrival is no reason to have to decorate with paper umbrellas and streamers. Instead, it should be a sophisticated, grown-up party, beautifully appointed with lacy linens and polished silver, and full of festive spirit that will give as much enjoyment to *all* the guests as it does to the guest of honor.

Sugar cubes with pastel rosebuds are a flourish for a fancy shower given for Sarah Taich.

When planning a baby shower, remember the extra touches, such as guest towels in the bathroom and fresh flowers in every room into which a guest might wander. Remember, too, to have favors at each place setting: heart-shaped scented soaps wrapped in tulle and tied with satin ribbon; a silver-plated baby spoon (great for serving jam or mustard) with a fancy bow; a rose with a Victorian tag inscribed with the mother's name; or small terra-cotta pots planted with tiny bulbs.

Fill the house with symbols of new life—a pot of spring blooms or a blossoming branch, or the first fruits of summer, like rosy red strawberries, tumbling out of a silver bowl. Pastels and pale colors—even pure white— usually make the most subtle color scheme for tablecloths, napkins, and flower arrangements.

The best showers are simple—a meal that shows some careful planning but isn't overly fussy (and that takes any dietary considerations of the mother into account), and time spent laughing and telling happy stories of other babies and other times, linking the mother-to-be with that great chain of women who, through the ages, have waited out those long months before the birth of a child. Chances are, she will treasure the memories and the opportunity to share her thoughts as much as any of the practical and fanciful presents that wait in the pile nearby.

Guests at Sarah's shower gathered around a table set on the terrace. Each dish in this simple and engaging menu was decorated with fresh flowers and fruits. At party's end, the guests took home African violets nestled in silver baskets, RIGHT.

A pink theme is carried through the meal, from a white Zinfandel wine to the pink undercloth to the Strawberry Soup.

STRAWBERRY SOUP

This soup makes a colorful appetizer or an unusual dessert for a summer meal.

2 pints strawberries
¼ cup brown sugar, packed
1 cup white wine
¾ cup sour cream
¼ cup heavy cream

Puree 1 pint of the strawberries in a food processor or blender. Add the brown sugar, white wine, sour cream, and heavy cream and process until smooth. Set aside.

Slice the remaining pint of strawberries. Add the sliced berries to the soup and refrigerate until icy cold.

Serves 6

CRANBERRY-ORANGE MUFFINS

Baked goods look more attractive in decorative shapes. I like to use a heart-shaped tin.

1 cup sugar
½ cup (1 stick) lightly salted butter
3 large eggs
1 teaspoon baking soda
1 cup buttermilk
2 cups all-purpose flour
½ teaspoon salt
Zest of 1 orange
Juice of 1 orange
1 cup cranberries, cut in half if large

Preheat the oven to 400°F.

Butter the heart-shaped muffin pans.

Cream the sugar and butter together until fluffy. Add the eggs and beat until smooth.

In a separate bowl, add the baking soda to the buttermilk. Sift the flour and salt together and stir into the sugar, butter, and egg mixture alternately with the buttermilk until just blended.

Combine the orange zest and juice in a food processor. Stir the juice and the cranberries into the batter. Spoon into the muffin tins and bake until golden brown, or about 12 minutes.

Makes 16 medium-size muffins

After lunch, coffee was served while the presents were opened. A pink rose graced the serving tray, OPPOSITE. Sugared almonds accompany many Italian celebrations such as weddings and christenings; dropping one or two in a flute of champagne, ABOVE, will cause a cascade of bubbles. RIGHT, mints ended the shower on a sweet note.

A shower is the perfect place for a sentimental gesture. One grandmother strung her pearls with the baby lockets of her three daughters, LEFT, and will pass the necklace on to her oldest granddaughter. Presents were piled in an antique wicker carriage topped with a parasol, BELOW. OVERLEAF: Special shower gifts include porringers, antique spoons, and colorful china cups.

THE LAYETTE

or centuries mothers have spent the months before their babies' births readying clothing and toilet articles for their newborn child. Necessity certainly drove them to their sewing needles to turn out the swaddling clothes (bands of cloth used to wrap a baby tight) and caps that, until well into this century, covered a baby's downy head. Every mother threaded hopes and wishes into the little clothes, along with stitches that were fairy-fine.

Babies' wardrobes included cloaks and knitted hose in the sixteenth century, small linen corsets and bonnets in the eighteenth, and, when swaddling fell out of fashion in the nineteenth century, flannel undershirts and binders for the baby's tummy. Always there were diapers, sometimes made from the father's worn-out linen shirts, or, more recently, Turkish toweling. Beyond these necessities, even the poorest mother would take care

Until this century, no babe went bareheaded; bonnets were simple or edged with face-framing frills.

Assembling a layette (the word comes from medieval French for small coffer) has been a time-honored task for centuries. Here is a suggested list of basics: 6 undershirts, 6 bodysuits, 6 diaper covers, 6 stretchie sleepers, 6 to 8 receiving blankets (yes, the baby really needs these for swaddling in the first weeks, and they are useful for all sorts of purposes later on), 2 sweater sets, 2 pairs of booties, 6 bibs, 1 hat, 4 hooded towels, 4 to 6 washcloths, and 1 comb and brush set.

to lay away a few things that were simply pretty—tiny white sweaters or a petticoat trimmed with store-bought lace.

Wealthy families, of course, lavished babies with richly ornamented clothes and accessories—great billows of freshly starched dimity and lace, rucked and tucked little bonnets beneath which eyes shone brightly, bedclothes cascading with trimmed and embroidered linen. Practicality was the least of their concerns, as long as the baby was protected from drafts.

Fortunately, today's mothers do not have to choose between the practical and the pretty, although there will still be the fancy dress or sailor suit destined to be worn only once, then tucked away for the next child or the next generation. Many mothers begin to gather things the baby will need immediately, but whatever the timetable, it is important to have most of the essentials laundered and stored by the time the baby arrives.

Filling drawers and wardrobes with all that a baby requires is part of the pleasure of anticipation. It is also a time for remembering traditions—either inherited or borrowed. This old Christian Dior lace dress from the 1930s was found in a flea market, and refreshed with washing and light starch.

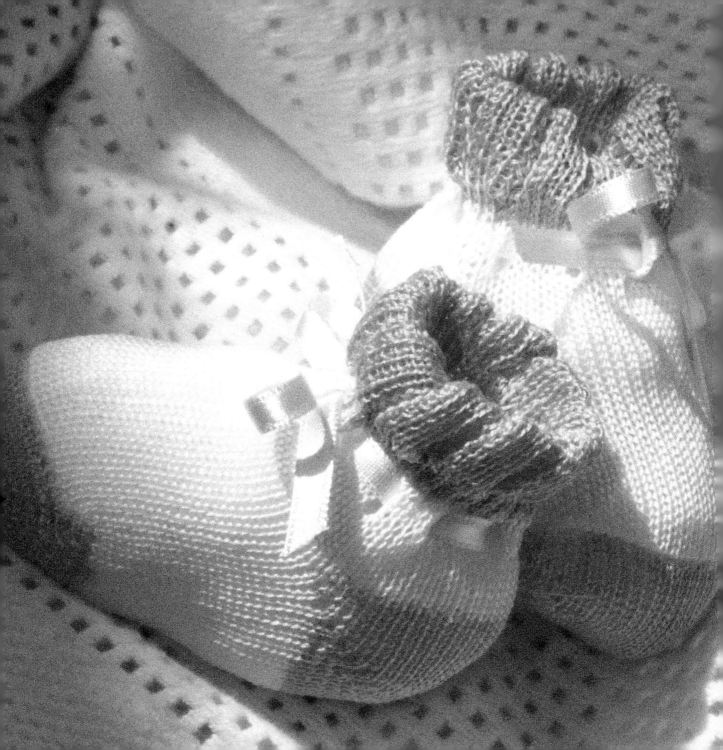

A few details make even the basics a pleasure. The cotton booties, OPPOSITE, *are trimmed with satin ribbon and are also practical. Cotton receiving blankets,* RIGHT, *are not only warm and washable, but, when wrapped snugly, comfort a newborn when nothing else will. Undershirts,* BELOW, *warm in winter, serve as outerwear in summer.*

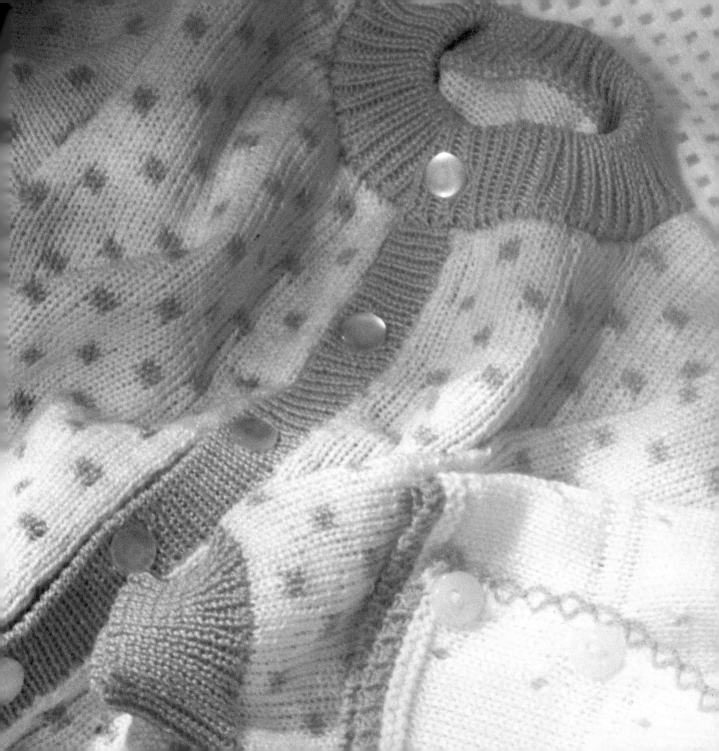

PREVIOUS PAGES:
Whether a prized gift or a mother or mother-to-be's own special purchase, small outfits are a delight. LEFT, *an Italian organdy day dress with soft lace and hand embroidery has a matching bonnet. A precious heirloom dress of lace is pretty enough to display in baby's room, long before she has grown large enough to wear it. Stretchies,* BELOW, *are the modern baby's daily basic.*

Every child needs a teddy bear, BELOW. Fancy baby dresses are a luxury, but such a delight that many mothers succumb to the indulgence. Smocked, laced, and ruffled, this Victorian day dress may be worn on a very special occasion, RIGHT.

An heirloom dress with tiny pink rosebuds is perfect for a new baby girl.

Tiny shoes, RIGHT, are a luxury, but sweaters, BELOW, are both necessary and traditional. Machine washable yarn makes the sweater practical; tiny ducks, bunnies, and nursery rhyme characters for the buttons make it special. A simple but charming project is the handkerchief bonnet, OPPOSITE. (See page 108 for instructions on how to make the bonnet.)

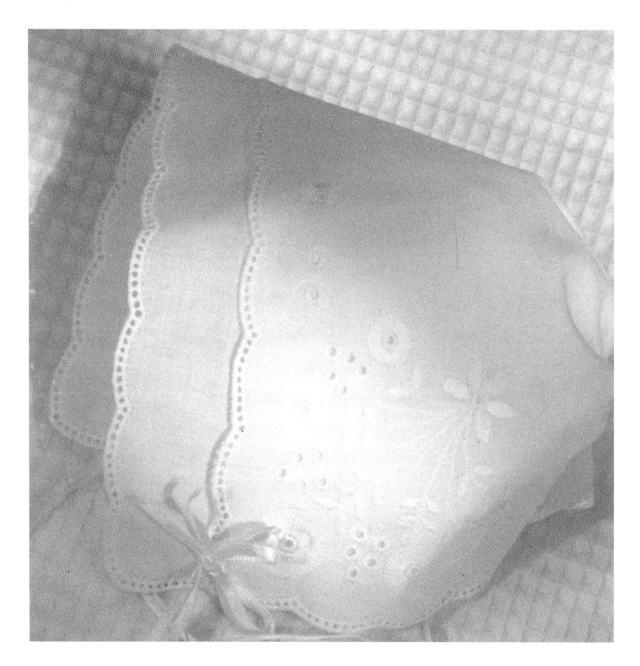

43

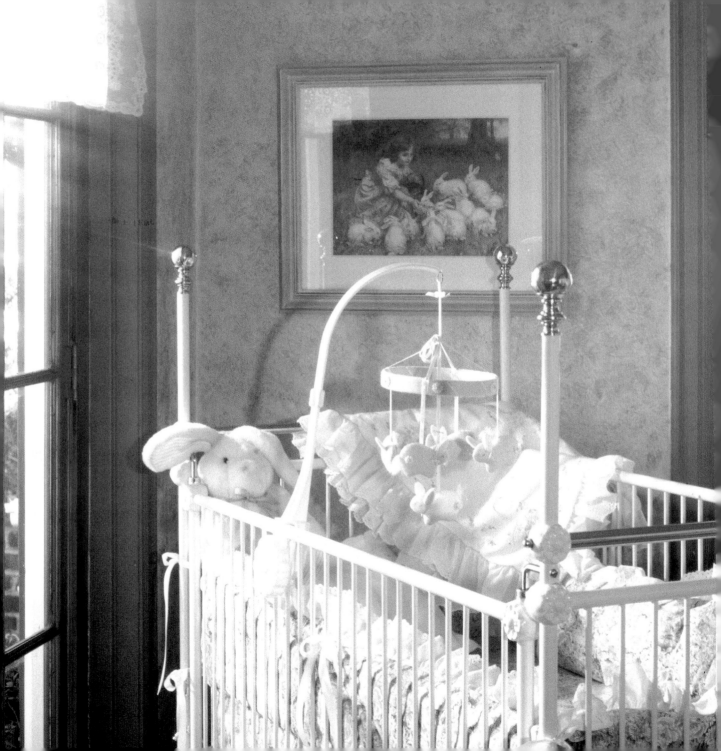

THE NURSERY

Whether the new baby comes home to a spacious nursery or a corner of the parental bedroom, the decorations and furnishings should suit the baby's needs and the parents' sense of style. Whether the space allotted for the baby is large or small, it should be furnished and decorated to be a special haven—comfortable and soothing for baby, yet pleasing to a parent's eye. As it was for Christopher Robin, the modern nursery is a child's own magic realm, partly invented by the parents from their own traditions and imaginations, but ultimately to be transformed by the particular new life that will make the room his or her own.

Fresh paint or paper, a warm rug on the floor, and curtains or blinds to dim the light at the window are the beginnings of a baby's new room. A crib is a necessity, a bassinet or cradle a luxury, and a changing table (possibly adapted

A room for a baby boy takes traditional toys as its primary theme.

One of the most wonderful kinds of furniture to collect for a nursery is child-size chairs. Victorians made many kinds of miniature chairs: tiny wicker rockers, rush-seated ladderbacks, Adirondack chairs, even upholstered wing chairs. Matched with an adult-size rocker in similar style, these old-fashioned chairs can create the foundation for a nursery decorating scheme. Avid collectors may find it difficult to part with these miniatures, even after baby has grown up.

from a chest of drawers of a comfortable height) and a portable changing station are useful items. For many mothers a rocking chair is essential—they treasure those memories of midnight hours rocking a small bundle.

Well-designed and handsome nursery furniture can be found in styles that range from simple to magnificent, but an older piece, whether passed along through the family or purchased at an antiques store, is not just functional, but meaningful. Refreshed with a new coat of paint and trimmed with eyelet or lace, the one-hundred-year-old bassinet is a comforting new home for the week-old infant. My favorite nursery style always has happy references to the past—favorite toys and objects brought down once again from the attic to bring back memories and inspire hopes for the future.

Through the ages, babies have often spent their first few months close to their parents' bed. The wicker bassinet, LEFT, dates from the 1920s. (Pillows must be removed when the baby is in bed.)

The bedside table, LEFT, holds mother's welcome-home bouquet, while another table in the bedroom, OVERLEAF, is full of mementos of babies past— a bronzed shoe, a mother-of-pearl teether.

A cabinet, like the antique wood one, LEFT, can be adapted to serve as a changing table, with a pad covered in fabric and a basket nearby to hold wipes and pins and powder. The whatnot shelf holds more baby supplies and a few beloved decorative objects—well out of baby's reach. The heart-shaped dried-flower wreath was a gift for the new little girl.

The traditional rocking chair is the place for lullabies, for teaching those first nursery rhymes, and for turning the pages of a favorite book, while wrapped in a soft woolly blanket. The turn-of-the-century wicker example, RIGHT, not only complements the pink-and-white scheme of this little girl's room, but is commodious and sturdy as well. Antique and modern rocking chairs come in many styles; there are even antique nursing rockers, built low to the ground so the mother can maneuver easily. Chairs with arms help mother or father support the baby, and long rockers give the slow gentle motion that is the most soothing to a crying child.

A soft pillow is useful for propping a baby and, personalized with initials and dates, can accompany the child into adulthood. The pillow, LEFT, is shadowstitched on cotton lawn, with pale pink lawn beneath, to give it a pastel tint. Victorian silver pieces, BELOW, can be transformed into containers for cotton balls and cotton swabs. The traditional canopy of the antique hanging cradle, RIGHT, resembles a bridal veil, with alençon lace and a circle of silk flowers at its crown.

The filmy layers of lace trim a bassinet.

Almost any room can be freshly translated as baby's own. The nursery, LEFT, was once a family library; its sponged moss green walls now serve as the backdrop for furnishings with an English country garden theme. A child-size table and chairs are painted to look like polite bunnies waiting for tea, and the tile floor and natural wicker chairs are reminiscent of an English garden room at the turn of the century. Flowers are everywhere, painted on the hutch, and fresh in a ribbon-tied vase, BELOW, adding their scent to the air.

This nursery, OPPOSITE, features traditional little-boy enthusiasms and a traditional blue-and-white color scheme, with ticking providing much of the powder blue. The antique iron models of old biplanes were found in a flea market. The Italian bassinet on wheels is filled with striped bedding, and the bedside lamp is shaped like a train. The changing table, ABOVE, is trimmed to match the bed.

The colorful clown, RIGHT, *performs a use- ful task at bedtime, playing the nightly lul- laby at a twist of a key. Childproof, from the firmly secured hat to the embroidered face, the clown music box is just the sort of soft toy that becomes a child's cherished, constant companion. A canopied crib,* OPPOSITE, *is a modern, romantic touch, its frills match- ing the eyelet bumpers and puffy quilt. The rocking horse of carved wood, sized to a two- year-old, is a decorative touch that will ulti- mately gallop off with a child on many adventures.*

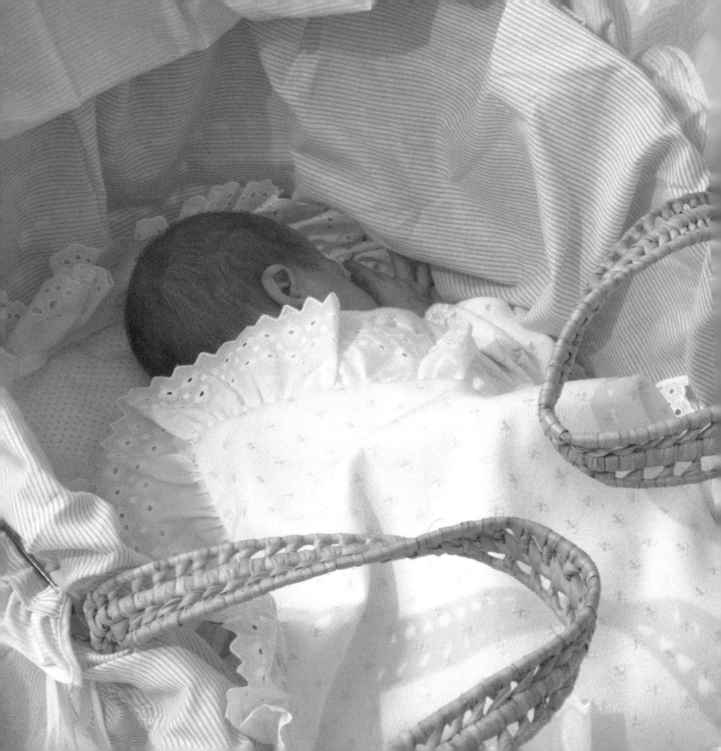

THE ARRIVAL

After the long months of waiting and dreaming, the flurry of preparation, and the excitement of the birth itself, the baby arrives at last, and it is time to rejoice. Every mother practices the ritual of counting tiny fingers and toes, cupping the small head in one's hand, stroking gossamer hair, and trying to determine just whose side of the family is responsible for those ears and that nose—all the rites of new motherhood, both private and public, that mark the beginning of a whole new world.

Sensitive new fathers can enhance the occasion and pamper their wives by filling the room with flowers, taking care of long-distance calls, and having camera and film ready for the first yawn and first sneeze. A charming old custom is the father's commemoration of a birth with a piece of jewelry for the mother—a sapphire ring at the birth of a boy, perhaps, or a ruby brooch at the birth

The arrival of a new baby is the occasion for passing on family heirlooms like silver cups.

Making the mother feel at home in the hospital is a wonderful way to begin the family's life with a new baby—even when it is a second or third (or fourth or fifth) child. Flowers are essential, along with a gift of new lingerie for the mother, and jewelry for mother or child or both! A picnic of favorite family foods, dressed up with linens and silver, sets a warm—even romantic—mood.

of a girl—or an antique selected from the family store of treasures. Brothers and sisters may enjoy bringing mother and the baby a flower or a handmade card—anything to make them feel they are part of the joyous occasion. (Most parents find that giving a small gift to the new arrival's brother or sister will ease those first fierce pangs of jealousy.)

Once women were hidden away after giving birth, and only began to receive callers after weeks of seclusion. A cradle or bassinet would be placed near the mother's bed, and she, dressed in her own laces, would receive her best women friends. Nowadays, friends and neighbors will visit the hospital, and a mother will value a pretty robe or bedjacket, a basket of soaps and creams and shampoo, or perhaps a flowery pillow slip to cover the hospital pillow. A corkscrew and glasses are essential to the hospital kit, in order to make the first toast to baby in appropriate style.

Try to reserve some time for just the two—or three—of you one evening. With a basket of favorite treats, a bottle of wine or champagne, china plates and cutlery, and a candle to set the mood, the family can reaffirm its bonds and celebrate the arrival of a new member.

The remarkable perfection of the new baby's hand, OPPOSITE, *never fails to inspire awe in parents and well wishers alike. Baby announcements can be found in a range of traditional and non-traditional forms— made by hand or custom engraved,* ABOVE.

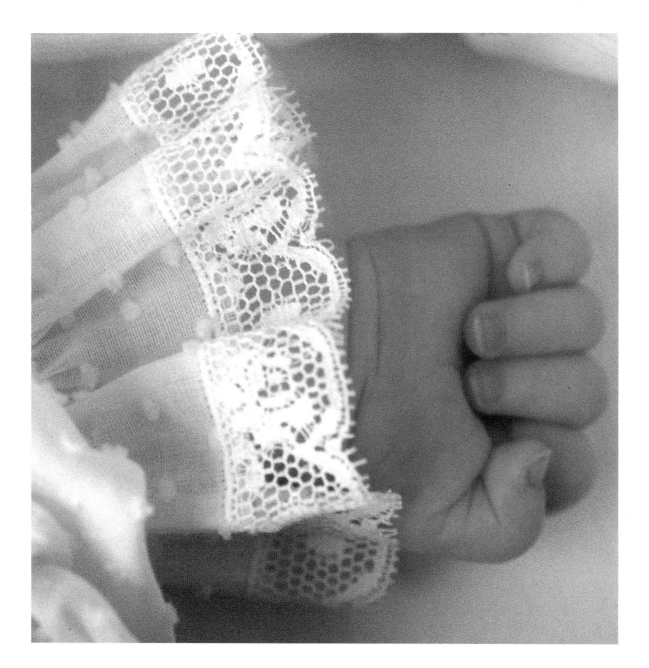

ITALIAN COUNTRY MEDLEY

Invented to rejoice in the birth of a baby to an Italian–American family, this dish travels well.

½ cup olive oil
2 large leeks, cleaned and thinly sliced
2 medium fennel bulbs, cleaned and thinly sliced
2 garlic cloves, minced
1 cup freshly grated Parmesan cheese
3 zucchini, sliced ⅛-inch thick
3 Japanese eggplants, sliced ⅛-inch thick
3 tomatoes, sliced ⅛-inch thick
Salt and black pepper

Preheat the oven to 375°F.

In a heavy pot, heat ¼ cup of the olive oil. Add the sliced leeks and sliced fennel. Cook covered for 15 minutes, or until tender but crisp. Remove from the heat and stir in the minced garlic.

Layer the bottom of an ovenproof serving dish with the leek and fennel mixture. Sprinkle with half the cheese. Add zucchini, eggplant, and tomato slices in concentric circles, then repeat the layers. Drizzle with the remaining ¼ cup olive oil. Add the salt and pepper to taste. Sprinkle with the remaining cheese. Bake for 45 minutes, or until the top has browned.

Serves 8

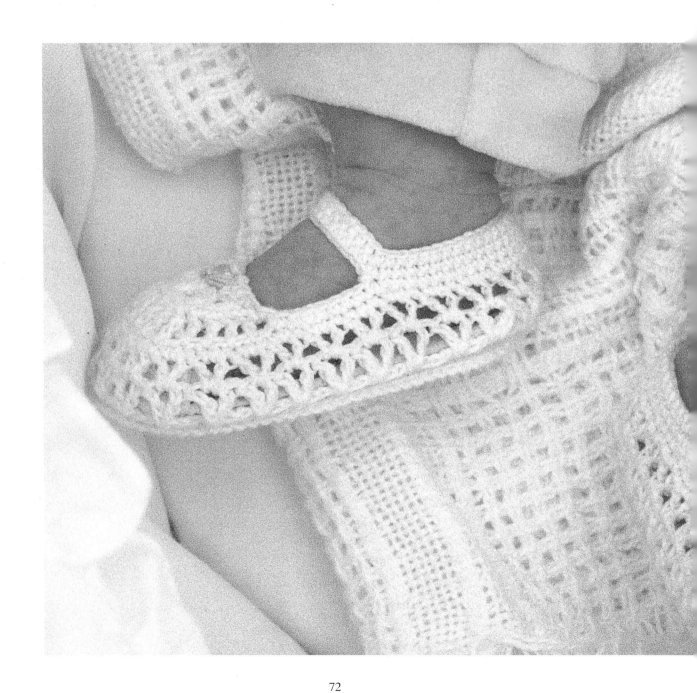

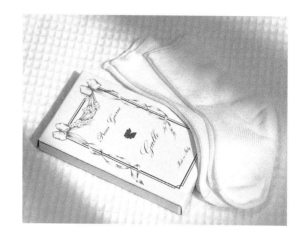

Knitted shoes, LEFT, *are soft on little feet, and an elegant variation on traditional booties. An old Italian custom requires a close family member to present a new baby with his or her first pair of socks, like the fancy cotton socks,* ABOVE, *along with a gift of money, for good health and wealth.*

THE WELCOME

very time and place has had its way of welcoming a new baby with a ceremony that connects the new arrival with family, religion, and community. In ancient Rome, friends and relatives would gather at the child's home eight or nine days after its birth to witness the child's official naming, and to recognize his or her parentage when the father raised the child from where it had been placed on the floor. Christian children are baptized within a few weeks or months of birth. A bris, the Jewish ritual of circumcision, always takes place eight days after a boy is born, while a girl is taken to the synagogue the first Sabbath after her birth and given her name there. And most families choose to crown the day with joyous festivities, reinforcing the spiritual ties with bonds of love and affection from friends, relations, and other well-wishers.

In Victorian times, a proper tea fol-

Welcoming a baby into his family and "tribe" is a custom practiced in many religions and cultures. Gifts for a christening should be the most lasting and traditional—silver cups with the child's name and birthdate, silver porringers, silver spoons and utensil sets, silver rattles, and jewelry—especially rings and tiny strings of pearls for baby girls. Even if the gift is monetary, it can be tucked into a gold-lined envelope, with a handwritten note.

Rustic furnishings on the lawn act as lectern and altar for a North Carolina christening.

lowed a christening. Spoons would tinkle in the cups as the smiling baby was borne in by his nurse in his elaborate christening dress. In village homes the whole community came for a feast, and the tables bent under the weight of cheese and hams and cakes. Today's welcoming receptions can be held at any time of day: a luncheon at home after a morning ceremony, a tea or cocktail party in the afternoon or evening. Parties that span the generations are especially enjoyable—with recognition of the family heritage as part of the theme. Godparents serve a special role, especially in this age of scattered families. The christening cake, traditionally all white, is decorated with the child's initials. And the champagne should be ready for the tender toasts to this tiny new life.

When James Whittaker Oates Warrington, Jr., was baptized in North Carolina, friends and family gathered near a lake. His bassinet was brought outside, so he could enjoy the day in comfort, RIGHT. Heirloom gifts honored the special day, LEFT.

Little girls, dressed in their best dresses and with flowers in their hair, find a moment for conversation, LEFT. *A christening luncheon traditionally seals the ceremony—and the Warringtons served favorite family dishes— along with champagne and mimosas to toast the newborn—at their buffet,* RIGHT.

LEMON CHICKEN SALAD

An outdoor buffet should be an array of foods that are easy to serve cold but are not monotonous.

FOR THE LEMON MAYONNAISE

1 cup mayonnaise, either homemade or prepared
4 tablespoons lemon juice
2 teaspoons dried tarragon
White pepper to taste

FOR THE SALAD

3 large chicken breasts, boned and skinned
1 cup heavy cream
2 cups cantaloupe chunks
2 cups whole seedless grapes
1 cup toasted slivered almonds
2 cups cucumber, peeled, seeded, and chopped
Zest of 1 lemon
¼ cup chopped fresh dill, or dried dill
1 teaspoon salt
1½ teaspoons freshly ground pepper

Combine all the ingredients for the mayonnaise in a small bowl and set aside.

Preheat the oven to 350°F. Place the chicken in an ovenproof dish and pour in the heavy cream. Bake for 20 to 25 minutes. Let cool. Shred the chicken into a bowl with the remaining ingredients and fold in the Lemon Mayonnaise.

Serves 12 as part of a buffet

WHITTAKER'S GREEN BEAN SALAD WITH VINAIGRETTE

In honor of Whittaker's French ancestry, his mother, Katie Warrington, created this marinated green bean salad, liberally seasoned with Herbes de Provence, found in specialty food stores.

2 garlic cloves, crushed
2 tablespoons Dijon mustard
1 cup olive oil
½ cup red wine vinegar
1 teaspoon fresh, crushed black pepper
½ cup chopped fresh parsley
¼ cup dried Herbes de Provence
2 pounds fresh green beans, ends removed
2 yellow bell peppers, julienned

For the salad dressing, combine the garlic, mustard, olive oil, vinegar, and black pepper and whisk well. Fold in the parsley and dried herbs. Set aside for several hours.

In a large pot, steam the green beans over boiling water until just crunchy. Rinse in cold water to stop the cooking. Drain and set aside. Put the beans and bell peppers in a large bowl and toss with the salad dressing. (Use as much dressing as you wish.)

Makes 1½ cups

Mimosas—good champagne with fresh orange juice—topped with a sprig of mint and orange slices, LEFT, were the special drink of the day. A christening cake, covered in white Royal icing, is the age-old favorite ending to the meal, but the Warringtons chose to serve small petits fours with Whittaker's initials piped in blue icing on top, BELOW.

THE FIRST
BIRTHDAY

A party for a child's first birthday marks a significant milestone—the official end of infancy and the beginning of childhood. First birthdays are often the occasion for a first haircut, with the precious curls rescued from the barber's—or kitchen—floor to be saved in an envelope. The one-year-old's grin is no longer toothless; her chubby feet are now planted firmly on the floor; and she seems to embrace these new attributes with a newfound, independent spirit.

The party that works best is often one that spans the generations—a few fellow toddlers, a few big sisters and brothers, and lots of grown-ups to help catch flying cake and enjoy the tumult. Of course, the children will be turned out in their best dresses and short pants and party shoes, and grown-ups will rise to the occasion, too. A simple lunch or tea will take nap time into

A single candle marks the end of the first exciting year—and the beginning of the next.

For a small child's birthday, there are three basic rules: keep the guest list small; keep the party hours short; and keep your eyes on the cake! Presents are best left wrapped until the guests have departed—to prevent the smallest guests from warring over new treasures. Personal touches, such as balloons printed with the birthday child's name, will make it an event to remember.

account. For little partygoers, just being there will be exciting enough, but you might think of a few simple games for the older children. Grown-ups will be happy with a glass of wine or champagne or a pretty punch (make sure it's out of the children's reach, however) and a menu that may suit adult palates more than children's. A plate of peanut butter and jelly sandwiches cut into animal shapes, however, should accommodate any "picky" eaters.

When the time comes, all eyes will be on the cake, so it should be a towering confection, with billows of icing and the requisite candle—as impressive as a wedding cake, though not as limited in flavors. As the birthday child grabs for the candle and everyone joins in the birthday song, it will have seemed only a moment ago that she or he entered the house, beginning that swift journey through childhood.

The first birthday party marks the dividing line between infancy and childhood—the end of one cycle and the beginning of another. Keara Stewart, clad in brand-new party shoes, OPPO-SITE, *and an heirloom lace dress, toddled from room to room, welcoming guests large and small to her informal celebration,* RIGHT.

BIRTHDAY HAM

1 whole country-smoked ham
Whole cloves
½ cup honey mustard
1 teaspoon dried ginger
½ cup honey
½ cup dark brown sugar, packed
2 cups apple juice
1 cup pineapple juice
1 cup Madeira wine
2 cups dried apricots
1 cup golden raisins

Preheat the oven to 350°F.

Peel the skin from the ham and trim the fat to a ¼-inch layer. Using a sharp knife, score the fat in a lattice pattern. Stud the ham with cloves.

Line a large, shallow baking pan with aluminum foil and place the ham in the pan, fat side up. Combine the honey mustard, dried ginger, honey, and dark brown sugar and pat it evenly over the top and sides of the ham. Pour the apple juice and pineapple juice into the baking pan. Cover the ham with aluminum foil and bake, basting frequently. When the ham has been in the oven for 1 hour, combine the Madeira, dried apricots, and raisins and add them to the baking pan. Continue to bake and baste the ham for 1 hour more.

Remove the ham from the baking pan and put it on a serving platter. Strain the dried fruits, reserving the basting juices as a sauce. Sprinkle the dried fruits over the ham. Serve immediately accompanied by the sauce.

Serves 12

PAM'S BISCUITS

2 cups all-purpose flour
¼ teaspoon baking soda
1 tablespoon baking powder
1 teaspoon salt
½ cup sugar
6 tablespoons solid vegetable shortening
¾ cup buttermilk

Sift the dry ingredients into a large bowl. Cut in the shortening until the mixture has a texture of coarse meal. Add the buttermilk and mix lightly but thoroughly. Add flour if the dough is too sticky. Knead for 1 minute. Wrap in wax paper or aluminum foil and refrigerate until well chilled.

Preheat the oven to 450°F.

Roll the dough out ½-inch thick on a lightly floured surface. Cut the dough into as many biscuits as you can. Bake on a dark baking sheet until golden, approximately 9 minutes.

Makes about 2 dozen biscuits

One, two, three—blow! Keara obliges for the camera, OPPOSITE, while the adults partake of coffee from the family's silver urn, RIGHT. Since most of the guests at a one-year-old's party will be adults, coffee and other sophisticated pleasures will make the occasion more enjoyable. The star of the menu was the birthday cake with its pale pink frosting and icing roses, OVERLEAF.

*By afternoon's end, ev-
eryone was ready for a
nap—especially Keara,
her brother, Sean, and
their parents. Each
guest left for home, BE-
LOW, with a tulle bag of
sugared almonds tied
with ribbon, RIGHT, a
souvenir of a memorable
day—and a memorable
first year.*

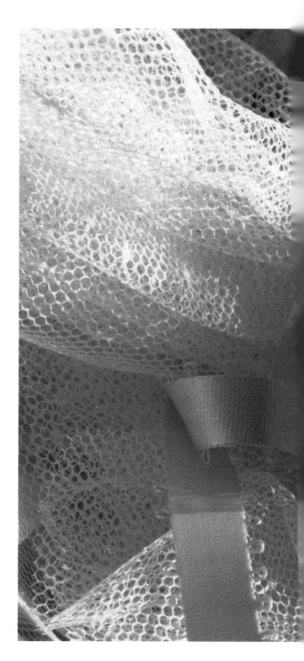

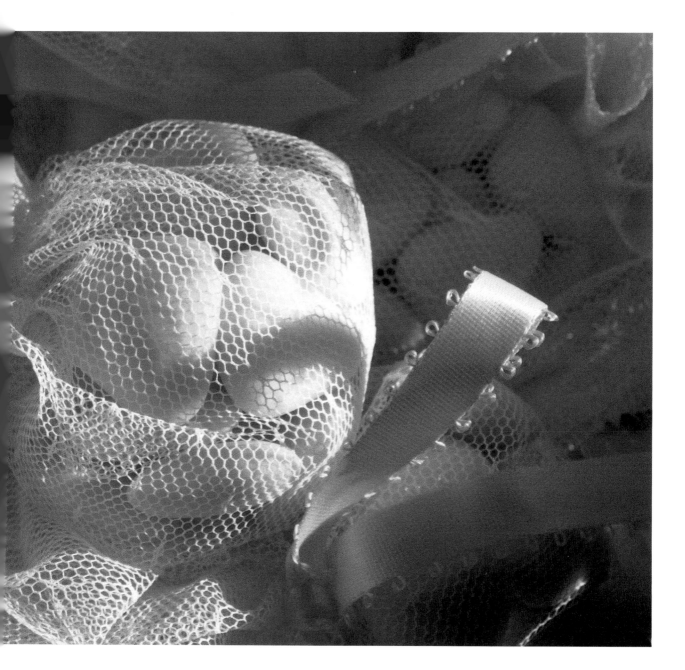

DIRECTORY OF SOURCES

For the best gifts for newborns and their parents and the most unusual favors for showers and birthdays,
try antiques stores and other unusual sources. Here are some of my favorites.

ALFIE'S ANTIQUE MARKET
13–25 Church Street
London NW8   England
(071) 723-6066
Antiques market with heirlooms suitable for shower, birth, and christening gifts for mother and baby.

ANDERSON GALLERY
721 Davis Street
Keene, NH   03431
(603) 352-7855
Nineteenth-century sterling silver cups and porringers.

AND OLD LACE
320 Court Street
Salem, OR   97301
(503) 585-6010
Antique lace and curtains to trim swinging cradles and nursery windows.

ANGEL AND THE LAMB
Boonsboro Shopping Center
Lynchburg, VA   24503
(804) 384-0029
Hand-embroidered and hand-smocked newborn and children's clothing; imported toys and dolls.

THE ANTIQUE CENTER AT HARTLAND
Route 5
Hartland, VT   05048
(802) 436-2441
Antiques market with heirlooms suitable for shower, birth, and christening gifts for mother and baby.

AS YOU LIKE IT
3025 Magazine Street
New Orleans, LA
70115
(504) 897-6915
Sterling silver cups, porringers, spoons, teething rings, and other gifts.

AUNT SYLVIA'S VICTORIAN COLLECTIONS
P.O. Box 67364
Chestnut Hill, MA
02167
Handcrafted Victorian lamps to add a special charm to the nursery. Catalogue available.

A BABY'S SECRET GARDEN
P.O. Box 20508
Rochester, NY   14602
(800) 776-MAMA
Elegant baby gifts and accessories for the nursery. Catalogue available.

A BASKET CASE
Wachussett Plaza,
Route 12
West Boylston, MA   01583
(508) 835-2250
Wicker baskets filled with gifts for baby and mother.

BEEKMAN ARMS ANTIQUE MARKET
Route 9
Rhinebeck, NY   12572
(914) 876-3477
Antiques market with heirlooms suitable for shower, birth, and christening gifts for mother and baby.

BELL'OCCHIO
8 Brady Street
San Francisco, CA   94103
(415) 864-4048
Nosegay frills, ribbons for shower or birthday party favors.

BERMONDSEY (NEW CALEDONIAN) MARKET
Bermondsey Street and
    Long Lane
London SE1   England
(071) 407-3635
Antiques market with heirlooms suitable for shower, birth, and christening gifts for mother and baby.

BOUTIQUE DESCAMPS
723 Madison Avenue
New York, NY   10121
(212) 355-2522
Bed linens and accessories for babies and infants.

BRIMFIELD FLEA MARKETS
Richard May
Route 20, P.O. Box 416
Brimfield, MA   01010
(413) 245-9271
Antiques market with heirlooms suitable for shower, birth, and christening gifts for mother and baby.

THE BRITISH TREASURE SHOP, LTD.
P.O. Box 248
Short Hills, NJ   07078
(800) 765-3500
Edwardian-era British reproductions: silver-plated picture frames and hand-blown etched bottles for baby's lotions.

THE BROWN-EYED SUSAN
47 Rockland Road
Trenton, NJ   08638
(609) 883-8940
Bris gowns, naming ceremony gowns, christening dresses, little girls' fancy dresses, and accessories.

CAMDEN PASSAGE
Islington
London N1   England
Antiques market with heirlooms suitable for shower, birth, and christening gifts for mother and baby.

CATHERINE HAGOOD
111 Mayfair Drive
Taylors, SC   29687
(803) 244-2985
Special bakery items, petits fours, and cakes.

CHARLOTTE MOSS & CO.
1027 Lexington Avenue
New York, NY   10021
(212) 772-3320
Accessories to augment a special nursery.

CHELSEAS
6 Boston Way
Asheville, NC   28803
(704) 274-4400
Baby books, soaps and other special gifts for new mothers, antique baby silver.

CHERCHEZ
Front Street
Millbrook, NY   12545
(914) 677-9013
Gift baskets and toiletries for the mother; antique linens to trim a baby's room.

CHILDREN'S BOUTIQUE
126 South 18th Street
Philadelphia, PA   19103
(215) 563-3881
Fine domestic and European infant and children's clothing; hand-knitted sweaters; antique European linens; handmade quilts.

CHRISTIANA'S ENTOURAGE
1015 Montana Avenue
Santa Monica, CA
90403
(213) 395-9002
Antique and reproduction wicker furniture; hand-painted baby furniture; lamps, clocks, and other accessories; christening gowns.

CHURCH STREET MARKET
Marylebone
London NW8   England
(071) 402-8848
Antiques market with heirlooms suitable for shower, birth, and christening gifts for mother and baby. Alfie's Antique Market nearby.

CLASSIC WHITE
P.O. Box 37526
Milwaukee, WI   53237
Elegant, all white baby accessories, handkerchiefs for making baby caps, pillows. Catalogue available.

CLOUD 10
450 South Country Road
Palm Beach, FL   33480
(407) 835-9110
Classic bassinets and room trimmings; layette service.

COTTAGE HEIRLOOMS
323 East Adams Avenue
Alhambra, CA   91801
(818) 281-9211
Heirloom-quality infant gowns—imported lace, Swiss batiste, Irish linen, silks. Can do reproduction work.

DALE LAMBERTY
4 Keene's Road
Westport, CT   06880
(203) 226-3273
Cakes (see cake pages 96–97), cookies, petits fours.

CHURCH STREET MARKET
Marylebone
London NW8   England
(071) 402-8848
Antiques market with heirlooms suitable for shower, birth, and christening gifts for mother and baby. Alfie's Antique Market nearby.

THE DANBY ANTIQUES CENTER
Main Street
Danbury, VT   05739
(802) 293-9984
Antiques market with heirlooms suitable for shower, birth, and christening gifts for mother and baby.

DEIRDRE AMSDEN
Studio 38A,
Colmans Court
45 Morris Road
London E14 6NQ
England
(071) 987-9569
One-of-a-kind designs for patchwork quilts and hangings.

DONNA BISHOP
110 East 9th Street, A665
Los Angeles, CA
90079
(213) 624-3779
Baby clothing, from coats to hand-knitted berets decorated with roses.

DOTTIE DOOLITTLE
3680 Sacramento Street
San Francisco, CA
94118
(415) 563-3244
Layette and baby gifts services.

DRAGON OF WALTON STREET
23 Walton Street
London SW3 2HX
England
(071) 589-3795
Handpainted baby furniture.

E. BRAUN & CO.
717 Madison Avenue
New York, NY   10021
(212) 838-0650
Baby pillows; monogramming available.

FILIGREE
1210 Yonge Street
Toronto, Ontario
M4T 1W1   Canada
(416) 961-5223
Pretty linens; exquisite Victorian-style gifts—especially pillows—for mother and baby.

FLEUR-DE-LYS
405B West Main Street
Waynesboro, VA   22980
(703) 943-2040
Bath and boudoir items for baby and baby's room.

FORGET-ME-NOT
Mission Street between
   4th and 5th Streets
P.O. Box 7318
Carmel, CA   93921
(408) 624-9080
Antique and new children's clothing and quilts; handpainted furniture and antiques.

GRANNY-MADE
381 Amsterdam Avenue
New York, NY   10024
(212) 496-1222
Infant and children's knitwear, hand- and loom-knit, domestic and imported.

GUMP'S
P.O. Box 890910
Dallas, TX
75389-0910
(800) 284-8677
Wonderful selection of special heirloom baby gifts of silver plate cups, plates, etc. Catalogue available.

HEIRLOOMS BY EMILY
P.O. Box 190
Myers Road RD #1
Glen Rock, PA   17327
(717) 235-0466
Heirloom and christening dresses. Catalogue available.

THE HUDSON ANTIQUES CENTER
536 Warren Street
Hudson, NY   12534
(518) 828-1069
Antiques market with heirlooms suitable for shower, birth, and christening gifts for mother and baby.

HUDSON STREET PAPERS
581 Hudson Street
New York, NY   10014
(212) 243-4221
Victorian cards and stationery for birth announcements and thank-you letters.

HUXLEY MANOR
Route 1, P.O. Box 25
Pickton, TX   75471
(214) 866-2319
Victorian-style laces for canopied cribs and bassinets. Free brochure.

J & J PROMOTIONS
Jill Reid Lukesh and
Judith Reid Mathieu
Route 20
Brimfield, MA   01010
(413) 245-3436
Antiques market with heirlooms suitable for shower, birth, and christening gifts for mother and baby.

JABBERWOCKY
310 East Main Street
Fredricksburg, TX
78624
(512) 997-7071
Old and new textiles; baby pillows; replicas of vintage designs and Victorian-style white picture frames.

JAMES ROBINSON
15 East 57th Street
New York, NY   10022
(212) 752-6166
Antique jewelry for the mother; sterling silver baby cups, rattles, porringers, etc.

JANE WILNER
5300 Wisconsin Avenue
Washington, DC   20015
(202) 966-1484

1353 Chain Bridge Road
McLean, VA   22101
(703) 506-1445
Linens; layettes; children's apparel; nursery furnishings.

JAN HAGARA CATALOGUE
The B & J Company
P.O. Box 67
Georgetown, TX   78626
(512) 863-8318
Romantic Victorian prints;
dolls; plates for shower or
birth gifts. Prints to adorn
walls of baby's room. Cata-
logue $5.00, refundable
with order of $40.00
or more.

JEAN HOFFMAN AND JANA STARR ANTIQUES
236 East 80th Street
New York, NY   10021
(212) 535-6930
Antique laces for an antique
swinging cradle and nursery
windows.

JOHNNY JUPITER, INC.
1185 Lexington Avenue
New York, NY   10021
(212) 650-1910
Tableware and party favors
for showers; stationery; folk
art and antique linens for
decorating the nursery.

JUBILEE MARKET
Covent Garden (on old
Covent Garden Piazza)
London WC2   England
(071) 836-2139
Antiques market with heir-
looms suitable for shower,
birth, and christening gifts
for mother and baby.

KATY KANE INC.
34 West Ferry Street
New Hope, PA   18938
(215) 862-5873
Antique baby clothes, in-
cluding christening gowns;
tablecloths for accent tables
in baby's room; laces for
swinging cradles and cur-
tains for windows.

KENTSHIRE COLLECTION
37 East 12th Street
New York, NY   10003
(212) 673-6644
Wonderful heirloom jewelry
for the new mother.

KINDERHOOK ANTIQUE CENTER
Route 9H
Kinderhook, NY   12106
(518) 758-7939
Antiques market with heir-
looms suitable for shower,
birth, and christening gifts
for mother and baby.

LACIES'
2212 Nine Oaks Drive
Kennesaw, GA   30144
Children's heirloom
clothing. Catalogue
available.

LADY PRIMROSE'S
2200 Cedar Springs
   Street
Dallas, TX   75201
(214) 871-8333
Classic Peter Rabbit items,
mugs, china, etc., and some
handpainted furniture.

LAURA ASHLEY
1300 MacArthur
   Boulevard
Mahwah, NJ   07430
(201) 934-3000
Romantic English floral
fabrics, wallpaper, furnish-
ings, and accessories for
baby's room. Shops
nationwide.

LAVENDER & LACE
656 North Larchmont
   Boulevard
Los Angeles, CA   90004
(213) 856-4846
Vintage linens, quilts, wall-
paper, yard goods, and area
rugs; pillows made from
vintage needlepoint; fabrics
for the nursery.

LAVENDER'S BLUE
1107 Montana Avenue
Santa Monica, CA   90403
(213) 458-2110
Custom layettes of flannel
and vintage fabrics; vintage
chenille crib bedding.

LINEN LADY
5360 H Street
Sacramento, CA   95819
(916) 457-6718
Lace curtains and handmade
linens for baby's room.

LINENS
Isabel Winsberg
Canal Place, Suite 159
New Orleans, LA   70130
(504) 586-8148
Wonderful linens for baby's
bed and bath.

LINENS & LACE
4 Lafayette Street
Washington, MO   63090
(800) 332-LACE
Romantic window dressings,
table covers, and pillows for
the nursery.

LORI PONDER LTD.
5221 Wisconsin Avenue,
   NW
Washington, DC   20015
(202) 537-1010
Bedding, books, pillows,
and other embellishments to
create a warm, enchanting
nursery.

LOVE GIFTS
8541 Melrose Avenue
Los Angeles, CA   90069
(213) 652-0733
*Gift baskets filled with
soaps, slippers, books, etc.,
for new mother and baby.*

LYLIAN
1514 Saint Charles
   Avenue
New Orleans, LA   70130
(504) 525-2020
*Very special, French-
stitched baby clothes, most
of lawn.*

MALINA
11163 Santa Monica
   Boulevard
Los Angeles, CA   90025
(213) 312-5347
*Fine domestic and imported
baby clothing and accessories.*

MARY SIMMONS
2727 East Second Avenue
Denver, CO   80206
(303) 355-3130
*Classic baby layette,
booties, and new christening
gowns.*

**THE METROPOLITAN
MUSEUM OF ART**
255 Gracie Station
New York, NY   10028
(212) 535-7710
*Jewelry and other gifts for
the new mother; announce-
ment and thank-you notes;
art and baby books.*

**THE MIDDLEBURY
ANTIQUE CENTER**
Routes 7 and 116
East Middlebury, VT
05740
(802) 388-6229
*Antiques market with heir-
looms suitable for shower,
birth, and christening gifts
for mother and baby.*

MIGNON
1522 Saint Charles
   Avenue
New Orleans, LA   70130
(504) 581-5192
*Layette items, gifts, special
occasion dresses.*

**THE MILLBROOK
ANTIQUE MALL**
Franklin Avenue
Millbrook, NY   12545
(914) 677-9311
*Antiques market with heir-
looms suitable for shower,
birth, and christening gifts
for mother and baby.*

**MONOGRAMMED LINEN
SHOP**
168 Walton Street
London SW3 2JL
England
(071) 589-4033
*Elegant baby pillows and
towels; monogramming
available.*

NIGHT GOODS
The Gallery at
Harbor Place
3000 Chestnut Avenue
Department 402
Baltimore, MD   21211
(301) 467-1015
*Fine linens, baby pillows,
and accessories.*

THE OLDE LACE STORE
14106 Ventura Boulevard
Unit 106
Sherman Oaks, CA
91423
(818) 508-7772
*Turn-of-the-century chris-
tening gowns and bonnets;
antique baby quilts and lace
crib covers; vintage lace yard
goods; handpainted wooden
picture frames.*

ON ANGEL WINGS
59 Swaggertown Road
Scotia, NY   12302
*Victorian jewelry for the
new mother; angelic home
accessories for the nursery.*

**THE PAWLING ANTIQUE
CENTER**
71 Route 22
Pawling, NY   12564
(914) 855-3611
*Antiques market with heir-
looms suitable for shower,
birth, and christening gifts.*

PETER DE WIT
21 Greenwich Church
   Street
London SE10 9BJ
England
(081) 305-0048
*Handcrafted toys; hand-
painted furniture and decorative articles.*

**PETER RABBIT &
FRIENDS**
Lincoln between Ocean
   and Seventh Streets
P.O. Box 5843
Carmel, CA   93921
(408) 624-6854
*All Beatrix Potter, from
furniture to porcelain to
baby bedding.*

THE PICCADILLY COLLECTION
5906 Sharon Hills Road
Charlotte, NC 28210
(704) 552-6757
Christening gowns; new canopy cradles.

PIERRE DEUX
870 Madison Avenue
New York, NY 10021
(212) 570-9343
Wonderful French Provençal fabrics for baby's bedding. Delightful huge rag doll to decorate the nursery.

PINE CREEK COMPANY
P.O. Box 508
Canby, OR 97013
(800) 628-5414
Wonderful, simple, 100-percent cotton baby clothes.

PLACE DES ANTIQUAIRES
125 East 57th Street
New York, NY 10022
(212) 758-9000
Antiques shop with heirlooms suitable for shower, birth, and christening gifts for mother and baby.

PORTOBELLO ROAD MARKET
Portobello Road
London W10 England
Antiques market with heirlooms suitable for shower, birth, and christening gifts for mother and baby.

PRIMROSE COTTAGE
6702 20th Avenue NW
Seattle, WA 98117
(206) 782-8232
Handmade pinafores and bonnets.

QUEEN ANNE'S LACE
1745 Chota Road
La Habra Heights, CA 90631
(800) 654-4052
Handcrafted Victorian-style brass lockets to start a Christmas tree collection for the new baby.

REBECCA EBERSHOFF, INC.
110 East 9th Street, B686
Los Angeles, CA 90079
(213) 622-9879
Imported heirloom-quality baby clothes and accessories.

RENNINGERS ANTIQUE MARKET
740 Noble Street
Kutztown, PA 19530
(215) 267-2177
Extensive antiques market with heirlooms suitable for shower, birth, and christening gifts for mother and baby. Held the last weekends of April, June, and September. To be placed on mailing list, write to: Renningers Promotions, 27 Bensinger Drive, Schuylkill Haven, PA 17972.

RHINEBECK ANTIQUE CENTER
7 West Market Street
Rhinebeck, NY 12572
(914) 876-8168
Antiques market with heirlooms for shower, birth, and christening gifts for mother and baby.

ROSEBUD CAKES
311 South Robertson Boulevard
Beverly Hills, CA 90211
(213) 657-6207
Elaborate, custom-designed birthday and shower cakes, e.g., a storybook-shaped cake adorned with a castle and tiny animals.

SARATOGA COUNTRY ANTIQUE CENTER
Route 29
Saratoga Springs, NY 12866
(518) 885-7645
Antiques market with heirlooms suitable for shower, birth, and christening gifts for mother and baby.

THE SERVANTS QUARTERS
4237 South Alameda Street
Corpus Christi, TX 78412
(512) 992-2840
Imported hand-smocked dresses and christening gowns.

SHADOW BROOKE FARM
150 South Road
Deerfield, NH 03037
(603) 463-5713
Hand-crocheted Victorian christening bibs and booties.

SILHOUETTE
15 East Market Street
Rhinebeck, NY 12572
(914) 876-4545
Vintage and new vintage-style infant clothing, christening gowns, bed linens, and baby pillows.

SIMS ROGERS
P.O. Box 701
Cambridge, MD 21613
(301) 228-8858
Wonderful accessories for baby's room; antique christening dresses.

S. WYLER
713 Madison Avenue
New York, NY 10021
(212) 261-1000
Antique sterling silver junior sets, porringers, and baby cups.

TASHA TUDOR COLLECTION
The Jenny Wren Press
P.O. Box 505
Mooresville, IN 46158
(317) 831-1044
Tasha Tudor Collection; prints, stationery, cards, and books. Catalogue available.

THOMAS K. WOODWARD
835 Madison Avenue
New York, NY 10021
(212) 988-2906
American baby quilts and other antiques for baby's room.

TIFFANY & CO.
801 Jefferson Road
P.O. Box 5477
Parsippany, NJ
07054-9957
(800) 526-0649
Sterling silver baby cups, rattles, and frames. Stores located in California, Washington, D.C., Georgia, Illinois, New York, Pennsylvania, and Massachusetts.

TROUVAILLE FRANÇAISE
305 East 63rd Street
New York, NY 10021
(212) 737-6015
Wonderful antique day dresses, christening gowns, hats, etc. By appointment only.

THE VICTORIAN PAPERS
P.O. Box 411352
Kansas City, MO 64141
(816) 471-7808
Nostalgic collection of birth announcements, shower invitations, stationery, gift wrap, and ribbons.

VILLAGE ANTIQUE CENTER
Franklin Avenue
Millbrook, NY 12545
(914) 677-5160
Sterling silver rattles, Bessie B. Gutman prints, and baby quilts.

VITO GIALLO ANTIQUES
966 Madison Avenue
New York, NY 10021
(212) 535-9885
Wonderful antique accessories to hold lotions, cotton balls, etc.; fabulous collection of frames.

THE WEDDING FANTASTIC
2323 Fillmore Street
San Francisco, CA 94115
(415) 765-1950
(800) 527-6966
Exquisite gifts for showers, christenings, etc. Catalogue $3.00, refundable with first purchase.

WESTMINSTER LACE
1326 5th Avenue,
Suite 646
Seattle, WA 98101
(800) 262-LACE
Finely woven imported laces; bedding, curtains, pillows for the nursery.

PAMELA SCURRY'S WICKER GARDEN
1318 Madison Avenue
New York, NY 10128
(212) 410-7000
Exclusive country-sophisticated, handpainted armoires and chests of drawers for nursery; antique wicker rockers and tables; brass and iron beds for the nanny and later for the child's or guest room; antique appliqué quilts for wall hangings or as throws on the adult rocker.

PAMELA SCURRY'S WICKER GARDEN'S BABY, INC.
1327 Madison Avenue
New York, NY 10128
(212) 348-1166
Fine, classic baby furniture and accessories; handpainted armoires designed by Pamela Scurry: chests of drawers, high chairs, rockers, etc., in a variety of themes: carousel, beau bears, trains, English garden Victorian dollhouse, soldiers, toys, etc.

PAMELA SCURRY'S WICKER GARDEN'S CHILDREN, INC.
1327 Madison Avenue
New York, NY 10128
(212) 410-7001
Exclusive Pamela Scurry children's clothing and accessories, including bris gowns, naming ceremony dresses, christening outfits, special occasion dresses and boys' outfits, and layette service.

WILD GOOSE CHASE
1631 Sunflower Avenue
South Coast Plaza Village
Santa Ana, CA 92704
(714) 966-2722
Antique baby quilts, children's books, and folk art toys and dollhouses.

WOLFMAN-GOLD & GOOD COMPANY
116 Greene Street
New York, NY 10012
(212) 431-1888
Antique tableware and paper doilies for trimming a special shower, christening, etc.

THE WOODEN SOLDIER
P.O. Box 800A
North Conway, NH
03860
(603) 356-7041
Fine children's clothing; Victorian collectibles. Catalogue available.

HANDKERCHIEF BONNET

Choose a large (at least 10 inches) pretty
batiste or lightweight linen handkerchief.
With the right side of the handkerchief
facing down lay a 12-inch length of ½-inch
satin ribbon along the hem. Turn the hem
up over the ribbon and sew a pocket seam,
taking care not to stitch the ribbon to the
fabric. Gather the fabric into a tight circle
to form the back of the bonnet, and tie
the ribbon into a bow. Cut two 12-inch
lengths of the same ribbon and sew one to
each of the two remaining corners of the
handkerchief. Decorate with ribbons sewn
into bows at the corners. See page 43.